Chinese New Year

Festivals Around the World

Hello, my name is Bao-Zhi.

When you see Bao-Zhi, he will tell you how to say a word.

What is a Festival?

A festival takes place when people come together to celebrate a special event or time of the year. Some festivals last for only one day and others

Some people celebrate festivals by having a party with their family and friends. Others celebrate by holding special events, performing dances or playing music.

What is Chinese New Year?

Chinese New Year is a spring festival that is mostly celebrated in China in January or February. Chinese people and their families and friends come together and celebrate the start of every new year.

Dragon dances are performed during Chinese New Year.

To celebrate this special time of year, Chinese people eat festive foods, set off loud fireworks and perform **traditional** dances. Chinese New Year celebrations usually last for eight days.

The Story of Chinese New Year

A long, long time ago there once lived a monster named Nian who lived in the mountains. Every year the terrible monster came down from the mountains and into the small village below.

The villagers were very scared of Nian because he ate all of their animals and tried to hurt their children. Every time Nian came down from the mountains, they hid in their houses to keep their children safe from harm.

One year, a wise old man came to the village. The villagers told him how Nian scared them. The wise old man protected the village for three nights until he had to leave. Before he left, he gave them some advice. "The monster is scared by the colour red and loud noises" he told them.

The next night, the villagers decorated their houses in red, made loud noises and set off fireworks to scare Nian away. Nian never ever came back to the village again and they were finally safe from the monster.

Family and Friends

Chinese New Year is a time when people come together to celebrate the new year with their family and friends. For many people it is the first time they've seen their family in a year.

Families celebrate by eating special food, playing games together and decorating their houses ready for the Chinese New Year celebrations to begin.

Festive Food

All the family come together on New Year's Eve to enjoy a festive feast, called **Nian Ye Fan**. Special dumplings filled with meat or vegetables, called *jiaozi*, are eaten after midnight.

A coin is hidden in one jiaozi, whoever finds it is said to have good luck for the rest of the year.

Bao-Zhi says:
NEE-AN- YEE FAN (Nian Ye Fan)
JY-AYE-AZ-I (Jiaozi)

Jiaozi

12

Cakes, biscuits and sweets are eaten during the festival too. A traditional cake made from rice flour, water and sugar, called **nian gao** is eaten at Chinese New Year.

Bao-Zhi says:
NEE-AN-GOW (Nian Gao)

Nian Gao

Gifts

Children are given gifts of money in red envelopes or packets. They are kept under their pillow and slept on for seven nights after Chinese New Year ends, to bring good luck.

Red Envelopes

Bao-Zhi says:
Guo Nian Hao means Happy New Year in Chinese! GOR-NEE-AN HOW

Mandarin Oranges

Other gifts, such as Mandarin oranges, chocolate and candles are also given between friends and families to celebrate the start of the new year.

Decorations and Firecrackers

Red Lanterns

Chinese people wear red clothes, paint their doors red and use **red lanterns** to decorate their homes. This is because the colour red is thought to bring good luck.

The colour red and loud noises scared Nian, the monster away from the villagers.

People put **firecrackers** covered in red paper outside their houses too. When they are lit, they make a loud banging noise. Both the colour red and loud noises are thought to scare away evil spirits.

17

The Lantern Festival

On the last day of Chinese New Year, there is a big celebration called the Lantern Festival. People decorate their homes and come out onto the streets with thousands of red paper lanterns.

Red lanterns are believed to bring good luck and happiness.

People fill the streets to enjoy the music, parades, acrobats and special dances that the Lantern Festival has to offer.

Bao-Zhi says:

Bu Bu Gao Sheng means 'good luck' in Chinese.
BOO BOO GOW SHUN

The Dragon Dance

The dragon dance is one of the many dances performed during the Lantern Festival. The tradition of dragon making began hundreds of years ago. They are usually made from paper, silk and bamboo and can take many months to finish.

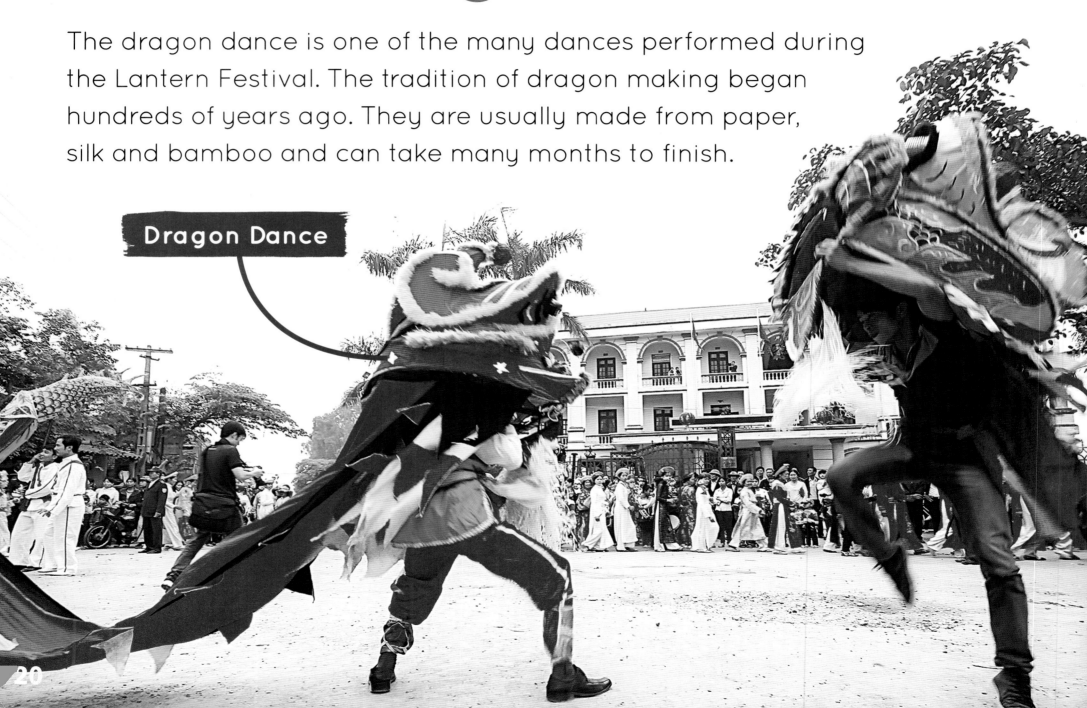

Dragon Dance

The dragon is held up by many performers who move its head and body, so it looks like it is dancing. The dragon dance is performed to scare away evil spirits and bring good luck in the new year.

Dragons used in the dragon dance can be over 100 metres long.

What Year is it?

There are twelve years in the Chinese calender that show the twelve Chinese zodiac signs. Each zodiac sign is named after an animal. The year you were born in, is your zodiac sign.

| Rat | **Ox** | Tiger | **Rabbit** | Dragon | **Snake** |

| Horse | **Goat** | Monkey | **Rooster** | Dog | **Pig** |

Each sign stands for something different. For example, people born in the year of the rabbit are said to be kind and loved. Ask an adult to help you find out which animal year you were born in.

Bao-Zhi Says...

Bu Bu Gao Sheng

BOO-BOO-GOW-SHENG

Bu Bu Gao Sheng means 'good luck' in Chinese.

Guo Nian Hao

GOR-NEE-AN HOW

Guo Nian Hao means 'Happy New Year' in Chinese.

Jiaozi

JY-AYE-AZ-I

Jiaozi are dumplings filled with meat or vegetables.

Nian Gao

NEE-AN-GOW

Nian Gao is a tradtional cake made from rice flour, water and sugar.

Nian Ye Fan

NEE-AN YEE FAN

Nian Ye Fan is a new year's eve feast.

Glossary

Firecrackers: a loud firework.

Nian Ye Fen: a New Year's Eve feast.

Red Lantern: a light covered in a ball made of red paper.

Traditional: something that is passed from person to person over a long time.

Index

Credits

Photocredits: Abbreviations: l-left, r-right, b-bottom, t-top, c-centre, m-middle. All images are courtesy of Shutterstock.com. Front Cover — L; Tom Wang R; tuthelens, 1L – Tom Wang, 1R – tuthelens, 2 – beltsazar, 4 – Tom Wang, 5 – Dragon Images, 7 – Dragon Images, 8 – Napatsan Puakpong, 8inset – leungchopan, 9 – manzrussali, 9inset – Sean Pavone, 10 – Dragon Images, 11 –XiXinXing, 12 – JIANG HONGYAN, 13 – aaekung, 14 – fotohunter, 15 – design56, 16 subin pumsom, 17 – cowardlion, 18 – 229394104, 19 – Rawpixel, 20 – Rawpixel, 21 – John Bill,